Diet recommendations for bile stones

Please check these recommendations always with a nutrition consultant, therapist, doctor or dietician. The recipes and the list of ingredients are supporting the conventional medical therapy.
The calorie disclosures of fresh ingredients (fruit and vegetables) vary according to quality and time of harvest. The contents were checked by a dietician and a nutrition consultant for the Traditional Chinese Medicine (TCM).

Author:
©2017 Josef Miligui
www.ebns.at

AF199920

Source:
The lists are created from the EBNS database for nutritional counseling. The database is used by dietitians, therapists and doctors for advising the patient / client.

Literature:
The specialist literature and the training documents of the German and Austrian dietary and traditional Chinese medicine serve as a knowledge base. We have used the documents as a basis of knowledge, adapted it to our experience and completed them.
http://di-book.com

Title Photo:
©2008 Erika Weixlbaumer

Production and publishing:
BoD – Books on Demand, Norderstedt
ISBN 9783746043043

Diet recommendations for DIETETICS - Gastrointestinal tract - Liver, gallbladder, bile ducts - Cholelithiasis (bile stones)

1   Treatment strategy

Eat 5 small fiber-rich meals daily.
Avoid large portions and fat meals and trans fats.
Avoid food which is suspected of causing bile collapses (fried foods, legumes, eggs, alcohol, coffee, black tea).
Sufficient liquid intake of at least 2 liters daily.
In case of pain, light normal diet.

2   Avoid

Overweight.
Fried, baked, roasted, healthy or breaded meat dishes, fat meats or poultry varieties such as goose, duck or fat pork, brain, brie, smoked bacon, kidney.

3   Breakfast

	kkal. per serving
Banana Soymilk	125
Barley mash with berries	112
Carrot and rice gruel soup	101
Celery juice	33
Celery soup	101
Compote from apples	67
Fennel-Rice Soup	155
Hearty polenta mash	262
Noodle soup - Also for babies from 10 month	236
Oat Congee	162
Potato cream with herbs and fresh cheese	217
Potato pancakes	893
Potato-basil soup	95
Pumpkin-yoghurt soup	68
Puréed banana	144
Rice congee with carrots and fennel	131
Rice dulse soup	190
Roasted millet with Celery sticks	400
Rosemary Potatoes	188
Soup with egg yolk	173
Strawberry yoghurt and almondpuree mix	134
Tea liver lather	0
Vanilla pudding	254
Whole milk cereal mash - Also for babies from the 8th month	205

4 Snack

5 Lunch

6 Afternoon

7 Dinner

8 Any time

9 Recipes

(recommendable) = You can use more.
(little) = You should use less than specified or omit.

9.1 Asparagus Cream Soup

Diuretic, improves blood circulation, prevents cancer, laxative,
antiparasitic, stimulates liver function, good to fight loss of appetite,
flatulence, rheumatism, heartburn.
Cooking time approx.45 min
Calories p. portion: 240
2 portions
Allergens: ACG

Quantity of ingredients:
Sour cream 15% fat 1 table spoon / 15g. (yes)
Asparagus (green or white) 5/8 oz / 200g. (recommended)
Water 2 cup / 500g. (yes)
Rapeseed oil 2 table spoons / 30g. (little)
Wheat flour 2 table spoons / 10g. (yes)
Cow's milk (whole milk 3.5% fat) 1 table spoon / 15g. (little)
Pepper (ground) 1 pinch / 0,5g. ()
Nutmeg 1 pinch / 0,5g. (yes)
Lemon juice 1 teaspoon / 2g. ()
Parsley 2 table spoons / 20g. (recommended)
Salt 1 pinch / 1g. (little)
Chicken yolk 1 piece / 25g. (little)

Cooking instructions:
Wash and peel the asparagus.
Heat water, a little lemon juice and pinch of salt till it boils. Tie the
asparagus spears together.
Add the asparagus peel to the cooking water and bring to the boil.
Add the asparagus and cook on low heat for about 20 minutes.
Then remove the asparagus bunches and pour the broth through a
sieve.
For the roux, heat the oil in a saucepan, add the flour and sauté until it
is colorless, slowly top up with the asparagus sauce and simmer for 10
minutes.
Cut the asparagus spears into pieces about 3 cm long and place them
to the soup.

Just before serving, bring the soup to the boil again. Mix the egg yolk

with the milk and sour cream.
Remove the pot from the heat and stir in the egg yolk and milk mixture.
Season with pepper and nutmeg, decorate with the chopped parsley
and serve immediately.

9.2 Banana porridge

Regulates gastrointestinal function. Protects the digestive system.
Detoxifying, affects anorexia, good to fight flatulence, inflammatory
bowel disease.
Cooking time approx.10 Min
Calories p. portion: 235
1 portions
Allergens: AG

Quantity of ingredients:
Water 1/2 cup / 125g. (yes)
Wheat flakes 1/2 oz / 20g. (yes)
Banana 1/4 lbs - 4oz / 100g. (recommended)
Butter Bio 1 table spoon / 10g. (yes)

Cooking instructions:
Mix the water with the flakes in a small pan. Bring to boil by low heat,
cook for 1-2 minutes and then remove from the cooking area. Cut the
banana in peace's into the pot, add the butter and puree with a blender.
Fill the banana porridge into a plate (feed the baby with the spoon).
(The afternoon porridge is basically cooked only with water, so it is all
the more important not to forget to add fat, otherwise your baby is
hungry long before the next meal.)
Instead of butter, you can also take corn oil - especially when the
porridge is not so hot, the oil is distributed more easily.
If you use buckwheat, millet, corn or rice flakes instead of wheat flakes,
the mash is gluten-free.

9.3 Banana Soymilk

Good to fight loss of appetite, oral mucosa inflammation. Strengthens
body energy, promotes stomach-spleen
harmony, promotes digestion, regulates gastrointestinal function.
Relieves pain, detoxifying, bactericide.
Cooking time approx.5 min
Calories p. portion: 126
2 portions
Allergens: E

Quantity of ingredients:
Banana 1 piece / 120g. (recommended)
Cinnamon ground 1 pinch / 1g. (yes)
Soybean milk 1 1/2 cups / 400g. (little)
Acerola fruit nectar or powder 1 teaspoon / 2g. (little)
Honey 1 teaspoon / 3g. (little)

Cooking instructions:
Cut the banana into pieces, puree them with soy milk, acerola, honey and cinnamon with the mixing stick.

9.4   Barley mash with berries

Diuretic, forcing spleen, supports urination, laxative, strengthens kidney, promotes digestion, detoxifying, promotes perspiration, reduces blood lipids, stimulates, dissolves stagnation.
Cooking time approx.2 hours
Calories p. portion: 113
5 portions
Allergens: A

Quantity of ingredients:
Raspberry 5/8 lbs - 8oz / 250g. (yes)
Ginger fresh 2 slices / 2g. ()
Cardamom 3 capsules / 1g. (yes)
Salt 1 pinch / 1g. (little)
Water 10 cups / 1200g. (yes)
Barley 1 cup / 120g. (yes)
Cocoa 1 pinch / 1g. (little)
Barley malt 1 table spoon / 15g. (yes)
Lemon Balm (fresh) 2-4 leaves / 3g. (yes)

Cooking instructions:
Boil the barley with water, ginger and cardamom pods in a large saucepan. Close pot with a lid and cook over low heat for about 2 hours.
For 2 servings of cooked barley porridge, place about 2 ladles in a bowl. Stir with sunflower seeds, malt, cocoa powder and a pinch of salt. Stir fresh berries into the porridge and serve sprinkled with fresh mint or lemon balm.

Tip: The pre-cooked barley porridge (without fruit) can be stored well in the refrigerator and used for sweet or savory dishes, e.g. with stewed vegetables or fruit seasoned compote.

9.5 Basic recipe for a beef broth (clear)

Strengthens muscles, tendons and bones, reduces blood pressure, strengthens immune system, prevents cancer, reduces radiation damage, stimulates digestion, reduces pain, promotes digestion, diuretic. Rosemary stimulates digestion.
Cooking time approx.4-8 hours
Calories p. portion: 114
10 portions
Allergens: O

Quantity of ingredients:
Beef soup meat 1,1 lbs / 500g. (little)
Clove 2 pieces / 2g. (yes)
Carrot 3 pieces / 210g. (recommended)
Juniper berry 8 pieces / 6g. (yes)
Leek 1 piece / 200g. ()
Anise (Common Fennel) 2 pieces / 1g. (recommended)
Vinegar (Red wine vinegar) 1 dash / 3g. (little)
Lovage 1 stem / 15g. (recommended)
Rosemary 1 pinch / 1g. (yes)
Water 3,3 lbs / 1300g. (yes)
Beef meatbones 5/8 oz / 200g. (little)
Pimento 6 pieces / 12g. (yes)
Salt 1 teaspoon / 5g. (little)
Parsnip 2 pieces / 300g. (yes)
Ginger fresh 1/2 teaspoon / 5g. ()

Cooking instructions:
Heat water, a dash of red wine vinegar, some juniper berries, a little rosemary, bones and meat till it boils; add carrot, parsnip, leek, ginger, lovage, clove, allspice, star anise and a little salt; simmer for 4-8 hours then strain.
Refrigerate for later use.

9.6 Basic recipe for a chicken broth worming

Strengthens blood, strengthens bone marrow, reduces blood pressure, strengthens immune system, prevents cancer, reduces radiation damage, promotes sweating, dissolves stagnation, good to fight loss of appetite,
Cooking time approx.2-3 hours
Calories p. portion: 90
9 portions
Allergens: L

Quantity of ingredients:
Chicken meat 1/2 piece / 600g. (little)
Water 4 cup / 900g. (yes)
Ginger fresh 2 slices / 2g. ()
Leek 1 stick / 45g. ()
Carrot 2 pieces / 150g. (recommended)
Juniper berry 1 teaspoon / 3g. (yes)
Fenugreek (Trigonella foenum-graecum) 1 teaspoon / 2g. (yes)
Bay leaf 3 pieces / 2g. (yes)
Celery root 1 piece / 500g. (recommended)

Cooking instructions:
Remove chicken parts from fat. Place chicken pieces in a saucepan with hot water and heat till it boils briefly, skimming any resulting foam. Add coarsely chopped vegetables and all spices and cook over medium heat for 2 to 3 hours. Strain the finished soup. Throw away vegetables and bones.
Tip: If you want to use the meat as a soup insert, take out after 45 minutes and return only the bones in the soup.
Refrigerate for later use.

9.7 Basic recipe for a reissue soup (Congee)

Low fat content, for the drainage of the body overweight and high blood pressure.
Cooking time approx.2-4 hours
Calories p. portion: 140
3 portions
Allergens:

Quantity of ingredients:
Rice variety any 1 cup / 120g. (yes)
Water 6 cups / 700g. (yes)

Cooking instructions:
Cook rice and water in a ratio of about 1: 6. The amount of water determines the thickness of the mash (matter of taste).
Put the rice in a saucepan with a heavy lid. It is important to simmer the rice after a short boil on the slightest flame, otherwise it burns.
Boil the rice for 2-4 hours. The longer he cooks, the more he strengthens.
If you want to eat the dish for breakfast, you can put the rice on just before bedtime.
To be on the safe side, you should first check the behavior of your pot and cooker under observation for a similar amount of time, so that nothing burns.
Refrigerate for later use.

9.8   Basic recipe for a vegetable soup, nutritious

Reduces blood pressure, strengthens immune system, prevents cancer, forcing spleen, dissolves stagnation, promotes weight loss. Good to fight immunodeficiency, high blood pressure, depressions, diabetes, diarrhea, reduces blood lipids.
Cooking time approx.2-3 hours
Calories p. portion: 48
5 portions
Allergens: L

Quantity of ingredients:
Parsnip 3/8 lbs - 6oz / 150g. (yes)
Lemon 1/2 piece / 25g. ()
Carrot 3 pieces / 200g. (recommended)
Celery root 1 cup / 100g. (recommended)
Salt 1 pinch / 1g. (little)
Juniper berry 6 pieces / 6g. (yes)
Onion white 1 piece / 60g. ()
Ginger fresh 1/2 teaspoon / 2g. ()
Olive oil 1 table spoon / 4g. (little)
Bay leaf 2 leaves / 1g. (yes)
Lovage 1 table spoon / 3g. (recommended)
Thyme dried 1 pinch / 1g. (yes)
Water 3 cups / 650g. (yes)

Cooking instructions:
Cut the vegetables into cubes.
Heat oil in hot pot, fry shortly onions and vegetables.
Add cold water, then add ginger, bay leaf and lemon juice.
Season with juniper, thyme and lovage. Cover for 2 - 3 hours on a low heat and simmer.
The used vegetables should be thrown away.
The basic recipe serves as a soup base and to refine vegetables, legumes or cereals.
If you want to eat vegetable soup immediately, add the desired vegetables half an hour before.
Refrigerate for later use.

9.9   Basmati rice + Zucchini tofu dish

Diuretic, supports urination, harmonizes spleen and stomach, reduces flatulence, good to fight body overweight and high blood pressure.
Antioxidativ, promotes digestion, perspiration, reduces blood lipids, forcing spleen.
Cooking time approx.20 min
Calories p. portion: 146
4 portions
Allergens: E

Quantity of ingredients:
Olive oil 2 table spoons / 6g. (little)
Zucchini 1 piece / 700g. (recommended)
Coriander 1/2 teaspoon / 4g. (yes)
Rice Basmati 1/2 cup / 60g. (yes)
Soy Tofu 5/8 lbs - 8oz / 250g. (little)
Water 3 cups / 200g. (yes)
Ginger fresh 1/2 teaspoon / 4g. ()

Cooking instructions:
Cut tofu cubes and marinate with olive oil, tamari, crushed coriander and ginger. Leave at least 1 hour.
Cook Basmati rice with the water. You can season with onion and cardamom.
Roast zucchini and tofu in pan in the hot oil for approx. 5-7 min.
Serve rice and tofu on a plate.
Add the parsley.
Can also be used as a salad for the home and on the go.

9.10 Carrot and rice gruel soup

Stops diarrhea, good to fight fever, strengthens immune system, reduces blood pressure.
Cooking time approx.10 min
Calories p. portion: 101
1 portions
Allergens:

Quantity of ingredients:
Carrot 2 pieces / 100g. (recommended)
Salt 1 teaspoon / 4g. (little)
Basic recipe for a rice soup (Congee) 1 cup / 120g. (recommended)

Cooking instructions:
Peel and grate carrots. Heat the rice soup (according to the basic recipe) till it boils and add the grated carrots and salt.
Cook for 10 minutes.

9.11 Celery juice

Mineral and vitamin rich, forces metabolism and dehydrating effect.
Cooking time approx.5 min
Calories p. portion: 33
1 portions
Allergens: L

Quantity of ingredients:
Salt 1 pinch / 0,5g. (little)
Water 1 cup / 120g. (yes)
Celery root 1/2 piece / 200g. (recommended)

Cooking instructions:
Peel celeriac and cut into pieces and juice. Mix with water and salt as needed.

9.12 Celery soup

Forcing spleen, calms nerves, stimulates appetite and digestion, dissolves stagnation.
Cooking time approx.45 min
Calories p. portion: 101
4 portions
Allergens: ACGL

Quantity of ingredients:
Nutmeg 1 pinch / 1g. (yes)
Salt 1 pinch / 1g. (little)
Butter Bio 1 table spoon / 15g. (yes)
Water 2 cup / 500g. (yes)
Celery root 1 piece / 500g. (recommended)
Chicken egg 1 piece / 55g. (little)
Cream sour 10% 2 table spoons / 25g. (yes)
Spelled wholemeal flour 2-3 teaspoons / 25g. (little)
Pepper (ground) 1 pinch / 0,5g. ()
Celery sticks 2 table spoons / 20g. (yes)

Cooking instructions:
In a hot saucepan, melt 1 tbsp butter; add a pinch of nutmeg, a pinch of salt, 1/2 cup wholegrain spelled flour (finely ground as fresh as possible) and stir to a sweat while stirring; add 1/2 liter of hot water gradually; add 1 large finely chopped celery tuber; cook for about 35 minutes and then puree; mix 1 egg yolk with 1 cup of cream; in the hot - no longer boiling! - soup vigorously; add some celery leaves finely chopped; with pepper, salt to taste.

9.13 Chicken soup with egg yolk and parsley

Strengthens blood, strengthens bone marrow, reduces blood pressure, strengthens immune system. Parsley stimulates liver function, harmonizes liver and spleen, strengthens eyesight, detoxifying.
Cooking time approx.10 min
Calories p. portion: 118
2 portions
Allergens: CL

Quantity of ingredients:
Chicken yolk 1 piece / 10g. (little)
Parsley 1 table spoon / 10g. (recommended)
Basic recipe for a chicken soup (warming) 2 cup / 500g. (recommended)

Cooking instructions:
Cook the chicken broth according to the basic recipe.
Heat broth and bubble the egg yolk. Sprinkle the chopped parsley over it and let it rest for about 2 minutes. Drink in small sips.

9.14 Chicken with white turnips on rice

Strengthens bone marrow. Rice to drain the body at overweight and high blood pressure.
Cooking time approx.45 min
Calories p. portion: 324
4 portions
Allergens: GL

Quantity of ingredients:
Garlic 2 pieces / 3g. ()
Rice Basmati 1 cup / 120g. (yes)
Turnips 4 pieces / 200g. (recommended)
Chicken meat 7/8 lbs / 400g. (little)
Olive oil 1 teaspoon / 4g. (little)
Salt 1 pinch / 1g. (little)
Parsley 2 table spoons / 15g. (recommended)
Basic recipe for a chicken soup (warming) 1 cup / 100g. (recommended)
Butter Bio 2 table spoons / 20g. (yes)
Olive oil 2 table spoons / 20g. (little)
Water 6 cups / 400g. (yes)
Onion white 1 piece / 60g. ()

Cooking instructions:
In a heavy pot, heat the butter and the oil at low temperature. Add the onion, stir and simmer for about 20 minutes on very low heat until soft and golden brown. Add the chopped beets and the chopped garlic cloves and stir well. Add the chicken broth or water, add some salt and heat till it boils. Reduce the heat, put on the lid and simmer the beets for about 20 minutes. Look in between if there is still enough liquid in the pot, and if necessary, pour in a few tablespoons of chicken stock. At the end there should be very little liquid in the pot. Remove the lid and allow the remaining liquid to evaporate, stirring constantly.

In the meantime roast the finely chopped chicken pieces in a frying pan with a little oil. Finally, sprinkle with a little chili and fry for another minute while constantly turning.
Serve the pieces of chicken, turnips and rice on the plates, spread the sauce over them and sprinkle with parsley immediately.

Cook the rice in the ratio of 6 cups of water: 1 cup of rice.
Small, fresh, untreated beets do not need to be peeled. Otherwise, peel

beets and place in hot water for 10 minutes. This makes them easier to digest and lose some of their sharp, pungent odor. White turnips are rich in vitamin C, potassium and folic acid.

9.15 Compote from apples

Apple (sweet) stops diarrhea, promotes digestion, appetizing, harmonizes the stomach. Warms stomach and spleen, improves blood circulation.
Cooking time approx.10 min
Calories p. portion: 67
2 portions
Allergens:

Quantity of ingredients:
Apple (sweet) 1 piece / 220g. (little)
Water 1 1/2 cups / 220g. (yes)
Cinnamon ground 1 pinch / 1g. (yes)

Cooking instructions:
Cook the apples (organic) with the skin and seeds. Sprinkle with cinnamon.

9.16 Fennel-Rice Soup

Forcing spleen, relieves constipation, stimulates nerves, detoxifying, reduces inflammation, improves blood circulation.
Cooking time approx.15-20 min
Calories p. portion: 156
2 portions
Allergens: EG

Quantity of ingredients:
Fennel 1/2 piece / 150g. (recommended)
Soy sauce 1 dash / 3g. (little)
Butter Bio 1 table spoon / 15g. (yes)
Basic recipe for a rice soup (Congee) 1 cup / 300g. (recommended)

Cooking instructions:
Cook the fennel softly in the rice soup according to the basic recipe. Before serving, add a piece of butter and some soy sauce.

9.17 Hearty polenta mash

Strengths spleen and stomach, promotes watering, promotes digestion, detoxifying, promotes perspiration, reduces blood lipids, stimulates, dissolves stagnation, stimulates appetite, dissolves stagnation.
Cooking time approx.10 min
Calories p. portion: 262
2 portions
Allergens:

Quantity of ingredients:
Salt 1 pinch / 1g. (little)
Onion (spring onion) 2 pieces / 40g. ()
Corn Grease (Polenta) 1 cup / 120g. (yes)
Turmeric (yellow root) 1 pinch / 1g. (recommended)
Ginger fresh 1/2 teaspoon / 2g. ()
Water 1 1/2 cups / 240g. (yes)
Olive oil 1 table spoon / 10g. (little)
Nutmeg 1 pinch / 1g. (yes)

Cooking instructions:
Stir in the polenta in boiling water and let it swell for 7 min. Add green onion, grated ginger, turmeric, nutmeg, salt and olive
oil and wait for 3 more minutes.

9.18 Kudzu soup in the morning

Many vitamins and minerals. Good to fight chronic coughing, asthma, diarrhea and thirst in diabetes mellitus.
Cooking time approx.5 min
Calories p. portion: 12
1 portions
Allergens: E

Quantity of ingredients:
Umeboshi paste 1 knife tip / 2g. (little)
Soy sauce 1 dash / 2g. (little)
Water 1 cup / 250g. (yes)

Cooking instructions:
Mix kudzu with cold water and heat till it boils while stirring. Once it is glassy, remove from heat and let cool. Season with Tamari and Umeboshipaste or crushed umeboshi plums

There is always the possibility to support your stomach and intestines with this recipe, taken before the right breakfast.
A morning cure for stomach and mucous membranes. Fix the base balance.

9.19 Melanzani with olive oil and turmeric

improves blood circulation, reduces inflammation, relieves pain, promotes digestion, helps to digest fat, supports urination, reduces blood pressure.
Cooking time approx.30 min
Calories p. portion: 432
2 portions
Allergens: A

Quantity of ingredients:
Turmeric (yellow root) 1/2 teaspoon / 1g. (recommended)
Ground 1 pinch / 1g. (recommended)
Tomato 4 pieces / 200g. (little)
Olive oil 4 table spoons / 60g. (little)
Salt 1 pinch / 1g. (little)
White bread (wheat bread) 4 slices / 80g. (yes)
Aubergine 2 pieces / 300g. (recommended)

Cooking instructions:
Cut the melanzani into slices and spread them with the tomatoes on a baking tray. Sprinkle with olive oil and then with turmeric, caraway and salt. Bake them in the tube 20 min.
Serve with the white bread.

9.20 Nettle-chard soup

Nettle promotes urination, detoxifies, supporting prostate disorders, reduces inflammation, analgesic. Chard supports intestinal activity, cleans intestine.
Cooking time approx.30 min
Calories p. portion: 52
4 portions
Allergens:

Quantity of ingredients:
Salt 1 pinch / 1g. (little)
Nettles Handful / 10g. (yes)
Pepper (ground) 1 pinch / 0,5g. ()

Chard 1 lbs / 500g. (yes)
Water 2 cup / 400g. (yes)
Olive oil 1 table spoon / 10g. (little)

Cooking instructions:
Heat the oil in a saucepan, add the washed and finely chopped Swiss chard. Salt and let simmer for 10 minutes. Add the chopped nettles and cook for another 10 minutes. Add pepper and puree.

9.21 Noodle soup - Also for babies from 10 month

Protects the digestive system. Detoxifying, affects anorexia, reduces blood pressure, strengthens immune system, strengthens the muscles, tendons and bones. stimulates liver function, detoxifying.
Cooking time approx.1 1/2 hours
Calories p. portion: 237
8 portions
Allergens: ACEGL

Quantity of ingredients:
Cauliflower 3/4 lbs / 300g. (little)
Beef soup meat 3/4 lbs / 300g. (little)
Tomato paste 1 table spoon / 10g. (little)
Water 4 cup / 900g. (yes)
Soy sauce 1 table spoon / 8g. (little)
Noodles (wheat) with egg 3/4 lbs / 300g. (yes)
Butter Bio 1 table spoon / 10g. (yes)
Bay leaf 1 piece / 1g. (yes)
Carrot 3/4 lbs / 300g. (recommended)
Salt 1 teaspoon / 2g. (little)
Celery sticks 1 bunch / 200g. (yes)
Parsley 1 Bunch / 100g. (recommended)

Cooking instructions:
Simmer the meat and bay leaf in the water over low heat for about 30 minutes.
Peel and slice the carrots.
From the celery plant separate the lower end and the leaves. Wash the stems, peel off the tough threads and cut the stems into slices about 1 cm thick.
Wash the Brussels sprouts, clean them and cut the roses from below crosswise.
Wash and chop the parsley.

Add the Brussels sprouts and carrot slices to the soup and cook for about 30 minutes.

After about 10 minutes, add the celery and green leaves and the pasta. Finally, remove the bay leaf and celery green.

(For the baby, remove about 200-250 g of carrots, celery and noodles with broth, squeeze about 35 g of meat finely and add to the baby soup, stir in the butter and 1 teaspoon of chopped parsley.)

Season the remaining soup with the salt, the soy sauce, the tomato paste and the remaining parsley. Lift out the meat.
Remove fat and bones and dice the meat. Serve in the soup.

9.22 Oat Congee

Strengthens immune system.
Cooking time approx.2-4 hours
Calories p. portion: 162
3 portions
Allergens: A

Quantity of ingredients:
Water 6 cups / 700g. (yes)
Oat 1 cup / 125g. (yes)

Cooking instructions:
Cook oats and water in a ratio of about 1: 6. The amount of water determines the thickness of the mash (pure matter of taste). The oats swell, so do not take much. Put the oats in a saucepan with good insulation and a heavy lid. It is important
to simmer the oats after a short boil on the slightest flame, otherwise it burns. Cook the oat for 2-4 hours. The longer it cooks, the more he strengthens.

9.23 Potato cream with herbs and fresh cheese

Good to fight loss of appetite, constipation, bloating and nausea.
Improves digestion, supports urination, prevents cancer, forcing spleen, dissolves stagnation, relaxing and reassuring.
Cooking time approx.25 min
Calories p. portion: 217
2 portions
Allergens: G

Quantity of ingredients:
Yogurt (natural, 1.5% fat) 2 table spoons / 45g. (yes)
Fresh cheese 3 oz / 80g. (little)
Dill 1/2 teaspoon / 2g. (recommended)
Salt 1 pinch / 1g. (little)
Pepper (ground) 1 pinch / 0,5g. ()
Black caraway 1 pinch / 0,5g. (recommended)
Basil (fresh) 1 teaspoon / 4g. (yes)
Chives 1/2 bunch / 50g. ()
Potato (mealy) 5/8 lbs - 8oz / 250g. (recommended)
Parsley 1 teaspoon / 4g. (recommended)

Cooking instructions:
Softly steam the potatoes in the pan, peel them and press through the potato press.
Mix cream cheese, yoghurt and herbs under the potatoes, season with salt, crushed black cumin and pepper.

9.24 Potato pancakes

Promotes spleen, reduces inflammation, improves digestion, regenerates skin, supports urination, calms
nerves and stomach, laxative, antiparasitic.
Cooking time approx.15 min
Calories p. portion: 893
1 portions
Allergens: ACG

Quantity of ingredients:
Cream sour 20% 1/8 lbs - 2oz / 50g. (little)
Salt 1 pinch / 1g. (little)
Herbs various 1 table spoon / 10g. (yes)
Rapeseed oil 2 table spoons / 20g. (little)
Salt 1 pinch / 1g. (little)
Wheat flour 1/2 oz / 10g. (yes)
Chicken egg 1 piece / 35g. (little)
Potato (mealy) 5/8 lbs - 8oz / 250g. (recommended)

Cooking instructions:
Grater the peeled potatoes finely, add the remaining ingredients, mix well and salt. Heat the oil and add small flat cakes to the pan with the spoon. Roast the potato pancakes on both sides crispy golden brown. Place them on the plate with sour cream, salt and sprinkle with herbs.

9.25 Potato-basil soup

Reduces inflammation, improves digestion, supports urination, lowers cholesterol, reduces blood pressure, strengthens immune system, prevents cancer, reduces radiation damage, antioxidativ, dissolves stagnation.
Cooking time approx.25 min
Calories p. portion: 96
4 portions
Allergens: L

Quantity of ingredients:
Basil (fresh) 1 Bunch / 50g. (yes)
Potato 4 pieces / 200g. (recommended)
Ground 1 pinch / 1g. (recommended)
Pepper (ground) 1 pinch / 0,5g. ()
Lemon 1 teaspoon / 3g. ()
Salt 1 pinch / 1g. (little)
Sugar cane sugar 1 pinch / 1g. (little)
Olive oil 1 table spoon / 10g. (little)
Garlic 1 clove / 3g. ()
Celery root 1 piece / 500g. (recommended)
Peppers powder 1 pinch / 1g. ()
Water 2 cups / 450g. (yes)
Carrot 2 pieces / 100g. (recommended)

Cooking instructions:
Peeled and chopped 4 medium potatoes in a pot of hot water and 2 chopped medium carrots, a piece of celery root, apinch of pepper, a pinch of ground cumin, crushed a small clove of garlic, a pinch of salt, 1 teaspoon of lemon juice, simmer until the Vegetables is soft.

Add 1 bunch finely chopped basil into one half of the soup and puree everything; stir in the other half of the basil; with rose paprika, a pinch of whole cane sugar, 1 tablespoon of olive oil or butter, freshly ground pepper, salt to taste.

9.26 Pumpkin-yoghurt soup

Relaxes, reduces blood pressure, strengthens immune system, promotes weight loss. Good to fight immunodeficiency, loss of appetite, flatulence, depressions, diabetes, diarrhea.

Cooking time approx.15 min
Calories p. portion: 68
4 portions
Allergens: GL

Quantity of ingredients:
Anise (Common Fennel) 1/4 teaspoon / 1g. (recommended)
Salt 1 pinch / 1g. (little)
Yogurt (natural, 1.5% fat) 3/8 lbs - 6oz / 150g. (yes)
Fennel seeds ground 1/2 teaspoon / 1g. (recommended)
Ginger fresh 1/2 teaspoon / 2g. ()
Hokkaido pumpkin 1,1 lbs / 500g. (recommended)
Basic recipe for a vegetable soup (nutritious) 1 cup / 300g.
(recommended)
Peppermint 2 leaves / 1g. (yes)

Cooking instructions:
Heat the vegetable broth (after the basic recipe) till it boils . Add diced
pumpkin, chopped ginger, crushed fennel seeds and anise. Bring the
soup to the boil and simmer for about 12 minutes until the pumpkin is
soft.
Remove soup from the heat. Puree the soup with the yoghurt with the
blender. Serve soup with finely chopped mint sprinkled.

9.27 Puréed banana

Eat 2 times a day, regulates gastrointestinal function
Cooking time approx.7 min
Calories p. portion: 144
1 portions
Allergens:

Quantity of ingredients:
Banana 1 piece / 150g. (recommended)

Cooking instructions:
Mix the banana with the fork or purée with a blender. Leave to brown for
at least 5 minutes.

9.28 Rice congee with carrots and fennel

Worms, forcing spleen, relieves constipation, stimulates nerves, detoxifying, reduces inflammation, improves blood circulation, reduces blood pressure, strengthens immune system, prevents cancer, reduces radiation
Cooking time approx.2 hours and more
Calories p. portion: 131
3 portions
Allergens: G

Quantity of ingredients:
Cardamom 1/2 teaspoon / 1g. (yes)
Butter Bio 1 teaspoon / 3g. (yes)
Carrot 2 pieces / 100g. (recommended)
Fennel 1 piece / 250g. (recommended)
Basic recipe for a rice soup (Congee) 2 cup / 500g. (recommended)

Cooking instructions:
Cook rice congee according to basic recipe.
Clean and cut carrots and fennel.

When carrots and fennel are cooked from the beginning, they serve wholesomeness. If added shortly before the end of the cooking time, taste and vitamins are retained.

Refine with butter and cardamom before serving.

9.29 Rice dulse soup

Promotes spleen and liver, reduces blood pressure, strengthens immune system. Good to fight blood circulation disorders, diarrhea, free radicals. Antipyretic. Vitamin C rich. Promotes the exchange of iron and calcium. Increases resistance to infectious diseases.
Cooking time approx.5 min
Calories p. portion: 190
2 portions
Allergens: L

Quantity of ingredients:
Basic recipe for a rice soup (Congee) 4 cups / 500g. (recommended)
Basic recipe for a vegetable soup (nutritious) 2 cup / 500g. (recommended)
Dulse (seaweed) 2 table spoons / 15g. (yes)

Cooking instructions:
Worm up a portion of pre-cooked basic recipe for a ricesoupe (congee) and a portion pre-cooked basic recipe for a vegetable soup.
Bake the dulse in the oven at 220 degrees for 3 minutes. Spread the crisp dulse over the rice.

9.30 Roasted millet with Celery sticks

Promotes spleen and kidney, diuretic, promoting metabolism.
Cooking time approx.30 min
Calories p. portion: 400
2 portions
Allergens: L

Quantity of ingredients:
Cress 1 teaspoon / 3g. (recommended)
Herbs various 1 table spoon / 10g. (yes)
Salt 1 pinch / 1g. (little)
Celery sticks 2 rods / 50g. (yes)
Water 2 table spoons / 30g. (yes)
Sage 3-4 leaves / 2g. (yes)
Millet 1 cup / 120g. (yes)
Water 1 1/2 cups / 240g. (yes)

Cooking instructions:
Roast millet briefly, pour over water, heat till it boils and let stand for 20 min. to swell.

Cut celery into small pieces and mix with water, salt and fresh herbs and cook for 10 min. Add to the millet. Sprinkle fresh sage or watercress over it.

9.31 Rosemary Potatoes

Reduces Inflammation, improves digestion, regenerates skin, supports urination, lowers cholesterol. Rosemary stimulates digestion, strengthens lung, promotes spleen and kidney, dries out.
Cooking time approx.30 min
Calories p. portion: 188
2 portions
Allergens:

Quantity of ingredients:
Salt (herbal) 1 pinch / 1g. (little)
Olive oil 1 table spoon / 10g. (little)
Rosemary 1 teaspoon / 2g. (yes)
Potato 6-8 pieces / 420g. (recommended)

Cooking instructions:
Cut the potatoes into halfs, apply a little olive oil on the cut surface, then salt, sprinkle 2 - 3 rosemary needles on the potatoes.
Place the potatoes on the baking tray and bake them in the preheated oven for approx. 25 minutes to 190°C/374°F.

9.32 Soup with egg yolk

Strengthens muscles, tendons and bones, reduces blood pressure, strengthens immune system.
Cooking time approx.5 min
Calories p. portion: 173
1 portions
Allergens: CO

Quantity of ingredients:
Basic recipe for a beef soup (warming) 1 cup / 250g. (recommended)
Chicken yolk 1 piece / 25g. (little)

Cooking instructions:
Warm the beef soup according to the basic recipe for a beef broth, warm it up and jell the yolk.

9.33 Strawberry yoghurt and almond puree mix

Good to fight acute or chronic constipation of the intestine.
Little laxative. Relieves pain, detoxifying, bactericide.
Cooking time approx.5 min
Calories p. portion: 134
3 portions
Allergens: GH

Quantity of ingredients:
Yogurt (natural, 1.5% fat) 5/8 oz / 200g. (yes)
Strawberries 1,5 lbs / 700g. (yes)
Almond puree 2 teaspoons / 6g. ()
Acerola fruit nectar or powder 1 teaspoon / 2g. (little)
Honey 1 teaspoon / 3g. (little)

Cooking instructions:
Puree yoghurt, strawberries, acerola, honey and almond paste in a blender.

9.34 Tea from elderberry blossom tea

Good, if you have a sore throat. Good to fight colds. Promotes urination, good to fight flu, urinary stones, concentration weakness, blackheads, hay fever, rheumatism. Strengthen the immune system, diaphoretic.
Cooking time approx.10 min
Calories p. portion: 7
4 portions
Allergens:

Quantity of ingredients:
Elderberry blossom tee 4 teaspoons / 12g. (recommended)
Water 2 cup / 500g. (yes)

Cooking instructions:
Heat the water till it boils and put it aside. Add elderberry blossom tee and 10 min. to let go. Sweet to taste with honey. Strain when pouring.

9.35 Tea liver lather

Calms liver and bile.
Cooking time approx.10 min
Calories p. portion: 0
2 portions
Allergens:

Quantity of ingredients:
Water 2 cup / 500g. (yes)
Liver smoothing tea 2 teaspoons / 4g. (yes)

Cooking instructions:
Heat the water till it boils and put it aside. Add 2 teaspoons of the tea mixture and stir for 10 min. to let go. Sweet to taste with honey. Strain when pouring.
1/2 cup before and 1/2 cup after eating

9.36 Vanilla pudding

Helps to fight constipation.
Cooking time approx.10 min
Calories p. portion: 254
2 portions
Allergens: G

Quantity of ingredients:
Cow's milk (whole milk 3.5% fat) 2 cups / 500g. (little)
Sugar white 1 table spoon / 12g. (little)
Pudding powder vanilla 1 package / 37g. (yes)

Cooking instructions:
Give 3-5 tablespoons of milk into a cup, bring the rest in a pot to boil.
Pour the powdered pudding into the cup and stir until free of lumpy. As
soon as the milk boils, add the mixture and simmer under low heat for
about 3 minutes. Divide into prepared bowls.

9.37 Whole milk cereal mash

Reduces Inflammation, antiallergic, has a stabilizing effect on the blood
circulation, lowers blood glucose and cholesterol.
Cooking time approx.20 min
Calories p. portion: 205
1 portions
Allergens: AG

Quantity of ingredients:
Fruit mix juice 1/2 oz / 20g. (little)
Spelled flakes 1/2 oz / 20g. (yes)
Water 1/4 cup / 50g. (yes)
Cow's milk (whole milk 3.5% fat) 3/4 cup - 6 oz / 200g. (little)

Cooking instructions:
Boil the milk with the wholegrain flakes and let it swell. Add the pureed
fruit.

Switch between wheat, oats and wholemeal spelled flakes, as well as
the fruits. So you get a variety of flavors.

10 Effects of food

10.1 Use ingredients: recommendable

Acai powder
Anise (Common Fennel)
Asparagus (green or white)
Aubergine
Banana
Banana (cooking banana)
Basic recipe for a beef soup
Basic recipe for a beef soup (warming)
Basic recipe for a chicken soup (warming)
Basic recipe for a fish soup
Basic recipe for a rice soup (Congee)
Basic recipe for a vegetable soup (nutritious)
Bitter Herb liqueur
Black caraway
Blackberry's
Blue mallow tee
Cantaloupe
Carrot
Carrot (Early Carrot)
Carrot juice without sugar
Celery root
Chamomile tea
Chervil
Chervil dried
Chinese pearl barley
Codfish
Cottage cheese
Cream 10% coffee cream
Cress
Crucian
Dill

Elderberries
Elderberry blossom tee
Fennel
Fennel seeds ground
Fennel tea
Fox nut, gorgon nut, makhana
Gourd
Ground
Ground caraway
Herbal tea mix
Hibiscus
Hokkaido pumpkin
Kudzu
Lamb's lettuce
Lily bulbs
Loquate / Japanese medlar
Lotus roots
Lotus seeds
Lovage
Mascarpone cheese
Parsley
Parsley root
Potato
Potato (mealy)
Pumpkin
Red beet
Spinach
Turmeric (yellow root)
Turnips
Watermelon
Wax gourd
Zucchini

10.2 Use ingredients: yes

Aloe juice
Amaranth
Amaranth Pops
Angelica root
Apple puree
Arrowroot
Artichoke
Baking powder
Balm
Bamboo shoots
Banchatee (green tea)
barberry
Barley

Barley flour
Barley grass powder
Barley grouts
Barley malt
Barley not peeled
Basil
Basil (fresh)
Batavia
Bay leaf
Berries of the season
Blackberry leaves
Blueberry
Borage

Boxhorn clover seeds
Bread roll
Bread with carob kernel flour
Breadcrumbs (wheat bread, bread roll)
Broccoli
Buckbean
Buckwheat
Buckwheat (roasted) Kasha
Bulgur (cereals)
Burdock root tea
Butter (half fat)
Butter Bio
Buttermilk
Calamari
Carambola (Star fruit)
Cardamom
Carob flour, St. john's bread
Celery sticks
Cereal coffee
Chamomile
Channa-Dal
Chard
Chicken egg white
Chickweed
Chicory
Chlorella (fresh water)
Chrysanthemum blossom tea
Cinnamon ground
Cinnamon sticks
Clove
Cod
Coix (seeds) YiYi Ren
Compote (fruits of the season)
Coriander
Coriander (fresh)
Corn
Corn (fast polenta)
Corn (roasted)
Corn flour
Corn Grease (Polenta)
Corn silk tea
Corn starch
Couscous
Cow's milk (1.5% fat)
Crab
Cranberry
Cranberry
Cranberry jam
Cranberry juice
Cream sour 10%
Creamer
Crispbread
Cumin (Caraway seed)
Curcuma

Curd cheese 20%
Currant (black)
Currant (red)
Currant (white)
Daisy
Dandelion (young plants)
Dandelion juice
Dandelionroots tea
Dashi
Dulse (seaweed)
Endive salad
Fenugreek (Trigonella foenum-graecum)
Feta cheese
Fig
Fish pieces mixed (fresh water)
Flounder
Flower pollen
Freshwater crab
Freshwater fish
Fruit tea
Galangal
Gelatin white
Gelee Royal
Gentian root
Gentian root tea
Ginkgo fruit
Ginseng
Ginseng root
Goat and sheep's milk
Goat cheese
Gooseberry
Green tea
Guava
Halibut (Flatfish)
Hawthorn
Herbs bitter
Herbs of Provence
Herbs various
Herbs wild
Hibiscus tea
Hijiki
Hyssop
Iceberg lettuce
Jasmine blossoms tee
Jellyfish
Juniper berry
Kalmus
Kefir
King Solomon's-seal
Kohlrabi
Kukicha tea
Kumquats
Ladyfingers

Lamb's lettuce
Lavender blossoms
Leaf salads (bitter)
Lemon Balm (dried)
Lemon Balm (fresh)
Lemongrass
Lettuce
Licorice root tea
Lime blossom tea
Liver smoothing tea
Lobster
Longane
Lovage seeds
Luo Han Guo fruit
Lychee
Lychee In Preserved
Lye roll
Mallow (Malva sylvestris) blossom tea
Mare's milk
Marjoram
Mediterranean fish (cod, plaice,
haddock, sea eel, mackerel)
Medlar
Millet
Millet flakes
Mineral water
Miso
Miso black (fermented)
Mulberry fruit
Mulled Wine Spice
Mullet
Mussels
Nasturtium (nose-twister or nose-
tweaker)
Nettles
Noodles (wheat) with egg
Noodles (wheat, lasagne) with egg
Noodles (wheat, ribbon noodles) with
egg
Noodles (wheat, spaghetti) with egg
Nori, purple seaweed, red algae
Nutmeg
Oat
Oat flour
Oat fusion (baby food)
Oat milk
Octopus
Octopus
Okra
Orange blossom
Oregano dried
Oregano fresh
Oysters
Papaya

Parsnip
Passion blssoms tea
Passion fruit
Pearl barley
Pearl barley
Peppermint
Peppermint tea
Perch
Pimento
Plaice
Pomegranate
Potato flour
Prickly pear
Processed cheese 12%
Pudding powder vanilla
Quince
Quinoa
Radicchio
Radish black
Radish leaves
Raspberry
Raspberry leaf tea
Red berry (without sugar)
Rhubarb
Ribworttea
Rice (fragrance)
Rice (Gaoliang / Sorghum)
Rice Basmati
Rice flour
Rice long grain rice
Rice malt
Rice mash
Rice noodles
Rice red
Rice round grain
Rice starch
Rice sticky
Rice sweet
Rice variety any
Romaine lettuce / lettuce salad
Rose blossom tea
Rose hip
Rose hip tea
Rose leaf tea
Rosefish
Rosemary
Rucola
Rusk
Rye
Rye flour
Safflower (Dyer's thistle / Hong Hua)
Saffron
Sage
Sago (cereals)

Salmon
Salsify
Sea buckthorn
Seacrab
Shark
Sheep's milk
Sheep's milk yoghurt
Shrimp
Shrimps
Skim milk powder
Slug
Sorrel
Sour cream 15% fat
Sour milk
Sour milk cheese 20%
Sourdough
Spelled flakes
Spelled grain
Spelled semolina
Spiny lobsters
Spurdog (spiny dogfish, Schillerlocken)
Star anise
Stevia (candyleaf, sweetleaf)
Strawberries
Sugar substitute (sweetener)
Supplementary nutrition
Sweet potato
Tarragon (Estragon)
Tea mixture uric acid lowering
Thyme
Thyme dried
Topinambur
Trout
Tsampa (roasted barley flour)

Turnip
Valerian
Vanilla
Vanilla pod
Vanilla powder
Wakame
Water
Water hot
Wheat
Wheat bulgur
Wheat flakes
Wheat flatbread/pita bread
Wheat flour
Wheat semolina
Wheat semolina for children
Wheatgrass juice
Wheatgrass powder
Whey
White bread (baguette)
White bread (pretzel sticks)
White bread (roll)
White bread (wheat bread)
White breadcrumbs
White dumpling bread (wheat bread cut into chunks)
Whitefish
Wild herbs
Wild strawberries
Wormwood herb
Yam root, yam root tuber
Yarrow
Yarrow tea
Yogi tea
Yogurt (natural, 1.5% fat)

10.3 Use ingredients: little

Acerola fruit nectar or powder
Agar agar (kelp)
Agave nectar
Apple (sour)
Apple (sweet)
Apple juice (natural cloudy)
Apricot jam
Avocado
Bean oil
Bearberry leaf
Beef fillet
Beef meat
Beef meat (calf)
Beef meatbones
Beef Oxtail pieces
Beef soup meat

Berry juice
Blackberry jam
Blueberry dried
Blueberry jam
Blueberry juice
Borage oil
Buckwheat whole grain
Capers in olive oil
Cauliflower
Caviar
Chestnut puree
Chestnuts
Chicken egg
Chicken meat
Chicken yolk
Clarified butter

Cocoa
Cooking oil
Corn germ oil
Cow's milk (whole milk 3.5% fat)
Cranberries
Cream sour 20%
Cucumber
Cucumber (bitter)
Cucumber (spicy cucumber)
Curd cheese 40%
Currant jam (black)
Currant jam (red)
Currant juice (black)
Currants (black)
Currants (red)
Dates dried
Dates red
Deer meat
Deer meat
Deer's Bones
Ducks egg
Edam cheese
Feta cheese
Fig dried
Fish innards
Fish remains
Fish sauce
Fresh cheese
Fresh cheese from soya
Fresh cheese with herbs
Fructose (glucose)
Fruit mix juice
Goat
Goose eg
Gouda cheese
Grape juice red
Grape juice white
Grapes red
Grapes white
Grapeseed oil
Grass carp
Green spelt
Herring
Honey
Hop
Horse meat
Kiwi
Kombu seaweed (Saccharina japonica)
Lamb bones
Lamb meat
Lamb shoulder
Linseed oil
Mackerel
Malt

Mango
Mango juice
Maple syrup
Margarine
Margarine (diet)
Mold cheese
Mozzarella
Multi-grain bread (gray bread)
Mustard seeds
Mutton
Mutton
Nectarine
Oat flakes roasted
Oat meal
Olive oil
Orange jam
Palm oil
Peaches
Peaches (canned)
Peanut oil
Pear
Pear juice
Pheasant
Pigeon
Pigeon egg
Pineapple
Pineapple (from a can)
Pineapple juice without sugar
Poppy
Pork ham
Pork ham cooked
Pork ham smoked
Pork knuckle
Pork meat
processed cheese 30%
Pumpkin seed oil
Quail
Quail egg
Rabbit
Rabbit (wild)
Rabbit meat
Raisins
Rapeseed oil
Raspberry dried (immature)
Raspberry jam
Salt
Salt (herbal)
Sesame oil
Soy flour
Soy noodles
Soy sauce
Soy Tofu
Soy Tofu smoked
Soybean milk

Soybean oil
Spelled (Dark) bread
Spelled wholemeal flour
St. Benedict's thistle, blessed thistle,
holy thistle, spotted thistle
Strawberry jam
Strawberry Juice
Sugar - icing sugar
Sugar brown
Sugar candy white
Sugar cane sugar
Sugar fructose - fruit sugar
Sugar glucose - grapes sugar
Sugar Milk Sugar
Sugar molasses
Sugar palm sugar
Sugar white
Sunflower oil
Thistle oil
Tomato
Tomato juice

Tomato paste
Tomato puree
Tonic Water
Truffle
Tuna
Turkey breast meat
Turkey ham
Umeboshi paste
Vanilla sugar natural
Vegetable juice
Vinegar (Apple vinegar)
Vinegar (Red wine vinegar)
Vinegar Aceto Balsamico
Vinegar Aceto Balsamico white
Walnut oil
Wheat germ oil
Wild boar meat
Yeast
Yoghurt vanilla
Yogurt (natural, 3.5% fat)

10.4 Do not use contra-acting foods

Adzuki beans
Agrimony
Almond
Almond marzipan
Almond milk
Almond puree
Anchovy / Sardine
Apricot
Apricot dried
Apricot nectar
Apricots
Apricots juice
Basic recipe for a duck soup
Beans (green, fresh)
Beef bone marrow
Beef heart
Beef heart (calf)
Beef kidney
Beef liver
Beef lungs (calf)
Beef stomach
Beer (alcohol-free)
Beer (alcohol-reduced)
Beer (Pils)
Beer (Top-fermented German dark
beer)
Bitter Lemon
Bitter liqueur
Bitter orange peel
Black beans

Black fungus mushroom
Black tea
Blackberry dried (unripe fruit)
Black-eyed peas
Blackthorn (Sloe)
Bocksdorn fruits (Fructus Lycii, Goji,
goji berry
Boletus mushroom
Brazil nuts
Brie cheese
Broad beans (thick beans)
Brown ale
Brussels sprouts
Bush beans
Butter beans white
Camembert
Campari
Carp
Cashews
Champignon
Chanterelle
Chenpi (chinese tangerine bowl)
Cherry
Cherry (sour)
Cherry compote
Cherry juice
Chicken Blood
Chicken heart
Chicken liver
Chicken stomach

Chickpeas
Chili (pod or ground)
Chinese cabbage
Chives
Chocolate
Chocolate (Diabetic)
Clementine
Clementines
Coconut fat
Coconut flakes
Coconut grated
Coconut meat
Coconut milk
Coffee
Cola drink
Cola drink (low calorie)
Cream (30% fat)
Cream sour 30%
Cream, sweet 30%
Crème fraiche cheese
Curry
Curry paste red
Deer's kidneys
Duck (heart)
Duck (slaughtered)
Dyer's broom herb
Eel
Eel smoked
Emmental cheese
Evening primrose oil
Fernet Branca (herbal bitter liqueur)
French beans
Gail plum
Garam Masala powder
Garlic
Ginger fresh
Ginger oil
Ginger powder
Ginseng liqueur
Goat and sheep's blood
Goat and sheep's brain
Goat and sheep's liver
Goat and sheep's stomach
Goose
Goose fat
Goose parts
Goose blood
Gorgonzola
Grapefruit (Pomelo)
Grapefruit dried peel
Grapefruit juice
Greengage
Hazelnuts
Honey wine (Met)

Horehound leaves
Kaki plum
Kidney beans (red)
Lamb kidneys
Lamb liver
Leek
Lemon
Lemon juice
Lemon peel
Lentils
Lentils black
Lentils red
Lentils yellow
Lima beans
Lime
Linseed
Linseed (crushed)
Lychee liqueur
Manioc flour
Martini
Mayonnaise 50%
Mayonnaise 80%
Mirabelle plum
Miso paste (soy bean paste)
Mixed Pickles
Morel (black, dried)
Morel, dried
Mu Erh Mushroom
Muesli
Mung bean
Mung bean sprouting
Mustard
Mustard Dijon
Mustard medium hot
Mustard sweet
Noodles (whole grain) with egg
Oat flakes (whole grain)
Olives
Olives green
Onion (shallot)
Onion (spring onion)
Onion read
Onion white
Orange
Orange dried peel
Orange grated peel
Orange juice
Orange peel
Oyster mushroom
Oyster shell powder
Parmesan
Peanut (roasted)
Peanut butter
Peanuts

Peas
Peas, green
Pepper (ground)
Pepper Cayenne
Pepper powder (hot)
Pepper white (ground)
Peppercorns
Pepperoni
Pepperoni, red, pitted, halved
Pepperoni, yellow, pitted, halved
Peppers
Peppers (rose peppers)
Peppers (sweet)
Peppers powder
Pickle
Pig blood
Pine nuts
Pinto beans speckled
Pistachios
Plum
Plum dried
Plums
Pork Bacon
Pork brain
Pork fat (lard)
Pork heart
Pork kidneys
Pork Lard
Pork liver
Pork lung
Pork marrow bones
Pork sausage (Bratwurst)
Pork skin
Pork stomach
Pork/beef sausage (smoked)
Pork's intestine
Prosecco
Psyllium seed
Puff pastry
Pumpernickel (dark bread)
Pumpkin seeds
Rabbit liver
Radish
Radish (white, green, purple-red)
Radish horseradish
Red cabbage

Red wine
Reishi mushroom
Rice (whole grain)
Rice black
Rice wild (nature rice)
Rum
Rye wholemeal bread
Sake
Sauerkraut (cuted cabbage fermented)
Savory
Savoy cabbage / kale
Sea cucumber
Sesame oil roasted
Sesame paste (Tahini)
Sesame, black
Sesame, white
Sherry (whine)
Shiitake, dried
Sour cherries
Soya Cuisine (soy cream)
Soybeans
Soybeans, black
Soybeans, blacks, fermented
Soybeans, yellow
Spirit
Sunflower seeds
Tabasco
Tangerine
Toast bread (whole grain)
Tomato dried
Trout (smoked)
Umeboshi plums (Japanese apricots)
Walnuts
Walnuts roasted
Wheat beer
Wheat bran
Wheat flour whole grain
Wheat/Rye/Gray-black bread with yeast
White beans
White cabbage
White wine
Whole grain bread
Wholemeal flour
Wild garlic (garlic spinach)
Wormwood
Yew nut

11 Herbs and their effects

11.1 Basil (fresh)

It has a beneficial effect on flatulence and nausea, relaxing and soothing. Good against emphysema, bronchitis, whooping cough, high blood pressure, headache, mouth odor, warts, hiccup, gout, migraine.

11.2 Nettles

Promotes urination. Tea or juice, cleanses the blood and the kidneys, supports prostate problems, inhibit the formation of inflammation, pain-relieving.

11.3 Dill

The medicinal and spice herb has an antispasmodic effect and stimulates gastric juice production. Good against flatulence. Antispasmodic for gastrointestinal discomfort.

11.4 Dyer's broom herb

The Herb is used as a diuretic (for the purge of water) and for digestion. Due to the side effects, birch leaves or dandelions are recommended rather than the Dyer broom, which have very similar effects, but are not toxic.

11.5 Hop

Calming, hormone-regulating, appetizing, strengthens the stomach and intestines, diuretic, pain-relieving and antispasmodic.

11.6 Coriander

The essential oils are appetizing, digestive, cramping and soothing in stomach and intestinal disorders.

11.7 Herbs various

Appetizing, lots of trace elements and vitamins

11.8 Cress

Diuretic, supports urination. Good against dry mouth, inner agitation, sore throat, diabetes, kidney stones, gastrointestinal complaints, lung problems, menstrual cramps or cancer.

11.9 Chives

Bactericide, prevents cancer, strengthens gastric juice production, promotes digestion and blood circulation, promotes growth, triggers stagnation.

11.10 Lovage

Stimulates digestion, reduces pain. Extracts of the root are used to flush out urinary tract infections and prevent kidney gravel.

11.11 Balm

Soothing effect, Good for insomnia, restlessness and upset stomach, Allergies, Asthma, Migraine, Flatulence, Headache, Rheumatism and mental tension. To strengthen after cold and infectious diseases.

11.12 Agrimony

Good against persistent rheumatism, bedwetting, some mouth sores and spleen disease. For the treatment of wounds and inflammations of the skin as envelopes.

11.13 Oregano dried

It has an anti-digestive, calming and nerve-strengthening effect, helps against cramping stomach and intestinal disorders. The ingredient Carvacrol has an anti-inflammatory effect.

11.14 Parsley

Stimulates liver function, detoxifies. Forces urinating. Relieves flatulence. Digestive and menstrual stimulating, birth-accelerating, memory-enhancing, blood-purifying, skin-smoothing.

11.15 Peppermint

Relaxes, frees the lungs and the nose (inhale), regulates the cycle. Stimulates bile flow and bile production, antispasmodic in gastrointestinal disorders, antimicrobial and antiviral.

11.16   Rosemary

Promotes digestion, relieves bloating, strengthens lung, spleen and kidney. Affects the circulation and nerves. Appetizing. Baths help against circulatory disorders as well as with gout and rheumatism.

11.17   Sage

Against yeast infections. The leaves have a digestive effect and are used in greasy foods. Antiperspirant effect. Helps to relieve coughing attacks. Dries out (TCM).

11.18   Black caraway

Detoxifying, immunoregulatory. In addition, the oil should stimulate the formation of bone marrow cells and generally protect body cells from viruses.

11.19   Thyme dried

Disinfecting. It stimulates the blod circulation, increases the appetite and helps to digest fat meat better. Strengthens lungs and spleen (TCM).

11.20   Lemon Balm (fresh)

Stimulating, antibacterial, encouraging, relaxing, antispasmodic, cooling, antipyretic, analgesic, sweat-inducing, virus-inhibiting. Good for colds, fever, flu, cough, bronchitis, asthma, loss of appetite, bloating, heartburn.

12 Basics of Nutrition

The basic principles of nutrition described herein are general recommendations. They are not aimed at a specific form of therapy. Recommendations concerning a therapy have priority.

12.1 Nutrition

Regular meals in a relaxed atmosphere. A warm breakfast is considered a good start into the day.
The main meals ought to be taken for lunch – supper in the early evening. Pay attention to feeling hungry or sated: don't eat too much nor remain hungry is the rule
Prepare the meals freshly from natural, regional products. Frozen, heat-conserved, industrially prepared or foodstuffs cooked in the microwave oven are rejected.
Choice of foodstuffs according to the season: more cooling food in summer, more warming food in winter.
Eat cooked food at least twice a day. Food and drinks ought to be lukewarm, never ice-cold or hot.
Raw vegetables, briefly cooked vegetables, freshly squeezed juices and mineral water are not recommended. Milk and dairy products are only included in the diet if they don't cause problems.
Don't use therapeutic recipes over a longer period without consulting your doctor or therapist.

Varied food
Enjoy the diversity of foodstuffs. Characteristics of a balanced nutrition are variety, suitable combination and a balanced quantity of rich and low energy foodstuffs (on one hand avoiding undersupply with essential nutrients and on the other hand to take to many undesirable substances).

A lot of Cereal Products - and Potatoes
Bread, pasta, rice, cereal flakes (best wholemeal) as well as potatoes contain almost no fat, but many vitamins, mineral nutrients, trace elements, roughage and secondary plant substances. These foodstuffs ought to be taken with low-fat side dishes.

Vegetables and Fruit – „Take Five" every day ...
5 portions of vegetables and fruit a day, as fresh as possible, briefly cooked, or maybe one portion as a juice – ideal as a side dish to every meal as well as snack between meals: Thus a lot of vitamins, mineral nutrients as well as roughage and secondary plant substances

Daily milk and dairy products
Milk and Dairy Products every Day, once or twice per Week Fish;
meat, sausages as well as eggs moderately. These foodstuffs contain
valuable nutrients like calcium in the milk, iodine selenium and omega-3
fat acids in saltwater fish. Meat is favorable due to its high content of
disposable iron and the vitamins B1, B6 and B12. Quantities of 300 – 600
g meat and sausage per week are sufficient. Prefer low-fat products,
especially in meat- and dairy products.

Low-fat and fatty Foodstuffs
Fat supplies us with essential fat acids and fatty foodstuffs contain also
fat-soluble vitamins. Fat is high in energy; therefore much fat in the food
may cause overweight, possibly also cancer. Too many saturated fat
acids may further a tendency for cardio-vascular diseases in the long
term. Prefer vegetable oils and fats (e.g. rapeseed-, olive-, soya-oils and
solid fats produced therefrom). Beware of invisible fat in meat- and dairy
products, pastry and sweets as well as in fast-food and convenience
foods. 70 – 90 g fat per day is sufficient.

Moderately Sugar and Salt
Take sugar and foods/drinks containing various kinds of sugar (e.g.
glucose syrup) only occasionally. Use herbs and spices as well as a little
salt creatively. Prefer salt containing iodine.

Plenty of Liquids
Water is absolutely essential. Drink 1-2 l liquids every day. Prefer water
(with or without gas) and other low-calorie drinks. Alcoholic drinks should
not be taken.

Tasty Dishes, carefully cooked
Cook the meals with as low temperatures and as short as possible, using
little water and fat – this preserves the original taste, keeps the nutrients
intact and prevents the production of harmful compounds.

Take time and enjoy the food
Take your Time and enjoy your Food
Eating consciously helps to eat right. The eye enjoys food, too. It's fun,
invites to enjoy varied dishes and stimulates the feeling of satiety.

Watch your Weight and stay in Motion
A balanced diet and a lot of exercise and sport (30 – 60 min/day) are a
healthy combination. The right weight furthers well-being and health.
Thermals, directional effectiveness, digestive power

There are various criteria for judging the effectiveness of herbs and foodstuffs.

The use of certain herbs and ingredients is based on observations of the effects on the body which these foodstuffs, herbs and spices show after having eaten them. The medical science has developed following system: Every ingredient or herb has a directional effectiveness. Furthermore, there are herbs which have a special effect on certain organs.

The basic condition for a healthy metabolism is to obtain sufficient energy from food and that the digestive process doesn't use too much energy.

An easily digestible meal makes content and sated, doesn't cause flatulence and fatigue after the meal. The perfect spices increase the healthiness of our meals. Very often, just small doses of herbs and spices will suffice. They are not used to make us sated, but to help our digestive organs to digest the food.

12.2 Recipes

The recipes list the ingredients to be used and the cooking instructions show how the dish is prepared. The list of ingredients shows the concerned quantities as well as the relevance for the therapy. If you find „less than mentioned", try to comply or find an alternative from the „list of recommended foodstuffs". Mostly it shall result just in a small change of taste when you simply avoid this ingredient.

Mild cooking methods: boiling, stewing, poaching, steaming
Strong cooking methods: barbecuing, roasting, frying, smoking
Balanced cooking methods: deep-frying, baking brick
Deep-freezing and warming in the microwave oven should be avoided (denaturalization).

12.3 Foodstuffs

Foodstuffs have an effect on body and soul like medicinal herbs, only a very much milder one. Dietary advice is mainly based on regional foodstuffs. The knowledge about the effects of each foodstuff and the knowledge, when which foodstuff shall be used, is based on the orthodox school of medicine. Use ecologic-organic products, if possible. As everything should be cooked for a long time due to a better digestability and very rarely eaten raw, the food agrees with everyone.

The classification of the foodstuffs according to their effect on the body is the basis in order to achieve a harmonious status of health.

Dietary advisors do not recommend certain foodstuffs for everyone. The individual diet is tailor-made for the individual constitution.

Buy only fresh and ripe fruit and vegetables. You ought to leave unripe fruit and vegetables and such with brown spots and wilted leaves behind in the market. In this case take deep-frozen goods (never ready-to-serve dishes!). Fruit and vegetables are deep-frozen immediately after harvesting and often contain more vitamins and minerals than the goods from the vegetable shelf. Whereas conserved or tinned goods contain very much less biological substances. Also, salt, sugar and others are mostly added to the latter. Never leave the foodstuffs in the water after washing them to avoid that many vital substances get drowned. Clean salads, fruit and vegetables immediately before serving.

Please make sure of the hygienic processing of foodstuffs. Clean your salads, fruit and vegetables carefully. When cooking with meat, prepare all ingredients first and then process the meat products. Clean the worktop and tools very carefully. Wooden surfaces ought to be treated with a mild disinfectant regularly in order to reduce germination.

Store fruit and vegetables separately, if possible. Harvested fruit and vegetables are still alive and emit e.g. ethylene gas, which makes other products ripen and age faster. Keep meat and fish in the closed packaging or store them in the fridge in closed containers.

12.4 Herbs

There are some basic rules for storing medicinal herbs. On principle, herbs must be protected from direct sunlight, humidity and heat.

Containers for the storage of herbs may be glasses, ceramic jars and even plastic containers. However, plastic is a rather unsuitable material and should only be a short-term solution. In case of glass containers, use a dark material.

Medicinal herbs cannot be kept for any long period. The shelf life of herbs is limited. However, it can be prolonged with suitable storage. The place should be dark, rather cool and absolutely dry. A wooden medicine cabinet, placed not directly next to a source of heat, would be ideal. Never buy large quantities of herbs so as not to have to throw them away. Label the container with the name of the herb and the date of harvesting or processing.

13 Other dietic-books

The following syndromes of dietetics, TCM or for a therapy supplement for cancer are available.

Dietetics

E001. Nutrition of the infant - baby food
E002. Nutrition during lactation
E003. Nutrition in old age
E004. Nutrition of children and adolescents
E005. Nutrition of athletes
E006. Light weight
E007. Pregnancy
E008. Full food

Protein and electrolyte - kidneys
E009. (hemodialysis) dialysis treatment
E010. Acute renal failure
E011. Chronic renal insufficiency
E012. Nephrotic syndrome
E013. Kidney stones (nephrolithiasis)

Gastrointestinal tract - pancreas
E014. Acute pancreatitis (inflammation of the pancreas)
E015. Chronic pancreatitis (inflammation of the pancreas)

Gastrointestinal tract - small intestine and large intestine
E016. Acute obstipation (constipation)
E017. Chronic obstipation (constipation)
E018. Colon irritabile
E019. Diverticulitis
E020. Acquired lactose intolerance (lactose malabsorption)
E021. Fructose malabsorption
E022. Glutensensitive enteropathy (celiac disease)
E023. Colectomy
E024. Short Bowel Syndrome

Gastrointestinal tract - liver, gallbladder, bile ducts
E025. Acute and chronic hepatitis (inflammation of the liver)
E026. Cholelithiasis (bile stones)
E027. fatty liver
E028. cirrhosis

Gastrointestinal tract - Stomach and duodenal intestine
E029. Acute gastritis
E030. Chronic gastritis
E031. Stomach bleeding
E032. Ulcus ventriculi and duodenal ulcer
E033. Condition after gastric surgery

Gastrointestinal tract - oral cavity and esophagus
E034. Stomatitis
E035. Esophageal carcinoma (esophageal cancer)
E036. Refluosophagitis (heartburn)

Special diseases
E037. Phenylketonuria (PKU)
E038. Rheumatic joint diseases

Metabolism
E039. Obesity (overweight)
E040. Diabetes mellitus
E041. Eating disorders (underweight)

Fat metabolism
E042. Hypercholesterolaemia (increased cholesterol level)
E043. Hepatic Encephalopathy

Heart and circulation
E044. Arteriosclerosis (arterial calcification)
E045. Heart insufficiency
E046. Hypertension
E047. Hyperuricaemia and gout

Changed nutrient requirements
E048. In case of fever
E049. For malignant diseases
E050. After burns
E051. Radiation and chemotherapy

CANCER
E100. Pancreatic cancer
E101. Bladder cancer
E102. Blood cancer (leukemia)
E103. Breast cancer
E104. Colorectal cancer
E105. Gastric cancer
E106. Kidney cancer
E107. Esophageal cancer

TCM
E200. Bladder - moisture heat in the bladder
E201. Bladder - moisture and cold in the bladder
E202. Bladder - emptiness and cold in the bladder
E203. Large intestine - external cold affects the large intestine
E204. Large intestine - moisture heat in the large intestine
E205. Large intestine - heat blocks the intestine II acute
E206. Large intestine - dryness of the colon
E207. Large intestine - Yang deficiency (cold)
E208. Heart - Blood insufficiency
E209. Heart - Blood stagnation
E210. Heart - Fire
E211. Heart - Hot mucus clogs the heart pores

E212. Heart - Cold mucus clogs the heart pores
E213. Heart - Qi deficiency
E214. Heart - Yang deficiency
E215. Heart - Yin deficiency
E216. Liver - Ascending Liver Yang
E217. Liver - Blood deficiency
E218. Liver - Blood stagnation
E219. Liver - Moisture heat in liver and gall bladder
E220. Liver - Fire
E221. Liver - Gall bladder Qi-Empty
E222. Liver - Cold in the liver meridian
E223. Liver - Qi stagnation
E224. Liver - Wind
E225. Liver - Wind with ascending liver Yang
E226. Liver - Wind with blood anemic
E227. Liver - Wind with extreme heat
E228. Lung - Qi deficiency
E229. Lung - Mucus-moisture in the lungs
E230. Lung - Mucus-heat in the lungs
E231. Lung - Mucus-cold in the lungs
E232. Lung - Dryness of the lungs
E233. Lung - Wind-heat attacks the lungs
E234. Lung - Wind-cold affects the lungs
E235. Lung - Yin deficiency
E236. Stomach - Bloodstagnation
E237. Stomach - Fire
E238. Stomach - Cold with liquid
E239. Stomach - Nutrition stagnation
E240. Stomach - Qi deficiency
E241. Stomach - Rebellious Qi
E242. Stomach - Yin Emptiness
E243. Spleen - Heat and moisture attack the spleen
E244. Spleen - Coldness and moisture affects the spleen
E245. Spleen - Qi deficiency
E246. Spleen - Qi deficiency + Declining spleen Qi
E247. Spleen - Qi deficiency + spleen does not control the blood
E248. Spleen - Yang deficiency
E249. Kidney - Heart and kidney no longer communicate
E250. Kidney - Jing deficiency
E251. Kidney - Kidneys cannot receive the Qi
E252. Kidney - Qi is not stable
E253. Kidney - Yang deficiency
E254. Kidney - Yin deficiency

For further information visit di-book.com.